for
Artists

by Yogiraj
Peter Ferko

illustrations by Rebecca Oliveira

Yoga for Artists
ISBN: 978-1539503453
© 2016 Peter Ferko
Illustrations © 2016 Rebecca Oliveira

I am grateful for the continued guidance I receive from my teacher, Yogiraj Alan Finger, who founded ISHTA Yoga and initiated me as a Yogiraj, or master, in this powerful lineage.

Information at www.peterferko.com

Contents

Quotable

I'm very grateful to the talented artists who provided the descriptions of their experiences with yoga that appear in this book. I encourage you to experience their artistic work as well.

Shailly Agnihotri, playwright and producer

Nancy Allison, dancer, choreographer, and filmmaker

Benj Gershman, bassist

Debra Granik, filmmaker

Irina Kruzhilina, costume designer

Puy Navarro, actor, writer, producer

Agatha Nowicki, actor

Rebecca Oliveira, artist and designer

Melissa Staiger, artist and curator

Peter Yanowitz, drummer and composer

Shailly, Nancy, Irina, Puy, and Rebecca are also ISHTA Yoga teachers.

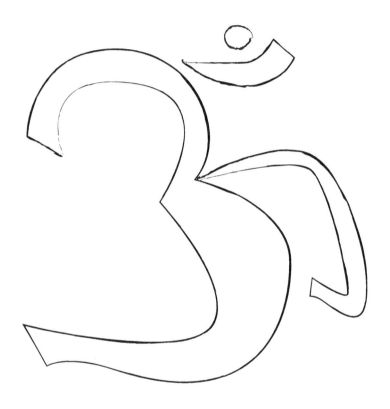

ॐ The sanskrit glyph, above, is Om, the yogi's name for the vibration emanating as the universe since its beginning. It is most often sensed as a humming or buzzing sound when the mind gets still. There is a parallel in science. Two scientists, Wilson and Penzias, were awarded the Nobel Prize in Physics in 1978 for determining that the hiss they were hearing in their radio telescope was the faint whisper of the Big Bang, or the afterglow that astronomers call the cosmic microwave background.

Chapter 1

Introduction

Why Yoga for Artists?

Artists are like warriors. They take on monumental challenges; accomplish them with remarkable skill, daring, and endurance; and rarely get the recognition they deserve.

Artists are like lovers. They give their all; they lay their hearts on the line; and they make work unconditionally, whether or not their love for the work is returned by the audience.

Artists are like shamans. They make something out of nothing, transform one's understanding of things, and move people from the mundane to the transcendent. They juxtapose opposites, integrate the separate, bring tears of joy and laughter of anger.

Yoga provides a way to become more skilled in facing challenge with calm and endurance; to become an unconditional lover of what life brings; and to navigate the realms of the creative and transcendent mind.

There are many disciplines of art and many genres within them. There are many kinds of artists. Some work solo, like painters, writers, or some recording artists; some work as part of a process, like choreographers, filmmakers, musicians in bands or ensembles, and composers. Creating art is a process that has phases: the idea phase; the experimentation phase; the compositional phase; the exhibition or performance phase.

Yoga provides a way to become more skilled in facing challenge with calm and endurance; to become an unconditional lover of what life brings; and to navigate the realms of the creative and transcendent mind.

Yoga is a practice that can help every kind of artist move gracefully through the immense challenges of creating, making, and showing or performing work. It does this by a process of doing without being attached to results; of self-study to undo patterns that don't serve you and to build approaches that do; and of surrendering to the source of creativity and wisdom we all have within.

In this book, we'll take a look at what yoga is, why you should practice it to help yourself as an artist, and how to practice in a way that suits you. If you already practice, good for you! You'll learn what gets left out of a lot of yoga classes and how to make the whole of yoga serve your art. I'll also share experiences from a number of artists I've had the privilege of teaching. I was inspired to hear how much practicing has helped them as artists; I hope you are inspired by them, too.

> Your intuition knows what to write, so get out of the way.
>
> ~ Ray Bradbury

My Story

I have had artistic experiences throughout my life that sent me so high that sometimes they made me cry, sometimes they made me laugh, sometimes they made me feel like I had found the meaning of life. I decided that making art was the way to find these feelings all the time. At first, the artwork I was making brought me tremendous satisfaction, but as the years went by, I became preoccupied with the business aspects of my chosen field, juggling money concerns, work, and relationships. I was saddened by the loss of the initial thrill of making work, of looking for beauty, love, and meaning in my art.

Then I noticed something interesting: I got the feeling back when I switched media. So I flowed between music, acting, visual art, curating, and writing, and each switch helped me refocus on the artmaking. I also found unique joy in each of the media, so I allowed myself to be a Renaissance man of an artist, rather than defining myself one way. I'm always intrigued when I see famous actors painting, musicians acting, or artists taking smaller bold steps to follow their intuitions about the next truth in their expressive journey.

I've lived in this city all my life … when I was [young] … all I thought about was art and music. Now, I'm 36, and all I think about is money.

~Wallace Shawn in
My Dinner With André

Early in my journey, I learned about yoga, which appealed to my philosophical nature. In the 1980's I studied ISHTA Yoga[1] at Alan Finger's yoga studio in Santa Monica. There were several celebrity actors and musicians taking classes at the studio, so I figured

---

1   See "About ISHTA Yoga," later in this chapter.

I had also found something valuable for my arts career. My career stayed more humble than some of my fellow students, but I started loving the yoga for itself. I began studying meditation at Self-Realization Fellowship on Sunset Boulevard near Malibu. I also read contemporary authors to gain a deeper understanding of the way the mind works, and studied yoga texts that my teachers suggested.

These studies helped me stay balanced in the emotional and highly competitive world I had chosen to enter. My life continued to be steered by attempts to find fruitful artistic pursuits, though those pursuits were challenging and making a living from art was always difficult.

I moved several times over the next decade and ultimately ended up in New York, where I was pleasantly surprised to find a yoga studio under the guidance of Alan Finger, who had also relocated from Los Angeles. I had tried a variety of yoga schools, but always longed for the authentic yoga practice I had found with ISHTA in Santa Monica, so I started studying ISHTA again in New York. I enjoyed my practice so much that I decided to take a teacher training program, though I had no interest in teaching. I knew the training would let me study more closely with Alan and my other ISHTA teachers and would help me better understand yoga and meditation practices. I thrived in the program and found I actually loved teaching, so I accepted an offer to teach classes at ISHTA. More than a decade later, with 30 years of yoga practice to draw on, I now train students who want to become teachers. I was honored four years ago to be initiated as a *Yogiraj*, or yoga master, by Alan Finger.

Teaching yoga became another facet in my life as a Renaissance man. And just as making a piece of visual art sometimes felt like writing a perfect song, teaching sometimes feels like a perfect performance, where I help students leave class in the same state I revel in when experiencing art. Yoga became a way for me to tap into more profound experiences that helped me in making and sharing art, and now I help other people have those experiences in their yoga practices, too.

I have recorded albums, received artist grants, curated shows, and published novels. None of that gained me celebrity recognition, nonetheless, all of those things are deeply important to me. At a point, I realized that major success for artists is rare — to use yoga vocabulary, it's only a few people's *dharma* to be working in the celebrity spotlight — and I no longer judged whether or not I was successful as an artist based on outside recognition, but on whether my life allowed me to make my artwork. With that shift in mindset, my yoga practice had not only helped me make art, stay balanced, and keep going, it had even helped me put things in a perspective that allowed me to work without being attached to the results.

I wrote this book, because I love to talk to artists about the most important part of art — not the logistics, technical minutia, or payoffs, but the reasons we make it, the search for meaning, the bliss of finding it. And because I see how yoga helps artists stay connected to that, I love to talk to artists about yoga, too.

About ISHTA Yoga

There are lots of "kinds" of yoga being promoted in the West these days. It's important to find the right kind of yoga to practice, so I devote a a whole section of *Chapter 4, How to Practice Yoga* to finding the right teacher, which will ensure that you get the right kind of yoga.

ISHTA Yoga is the school, or "lineage," that I learned and teach in. I love ISHTA Yoga, because it is an authentic practice that includes all the aspects of yoga, while taking into account the unique qualities and needs of each student. In fact, the word *ishta,* in Sanskrit, means the energy you, individually, need to reach your potential.

When I mention *yoga* throughout this book, I mean to distinguish an authentic yoga practice from yoga practiced only as a contemporary fitness or acrobatics routine, without any attention to the other aspects of yoga explained in the rest of this book. I'll start right in, on the next page, to help clear up common confusions and set you on the right path.

If you happen to find a good teacher who comes from a different school, everything I've written here should apply perfectly. A good teacher should be able to discuss anything in this book with you to tailor it to your individual needs as an artist. If your current teacher doesn't include something you read about here, you can ask if it's possible to include that in practice — like musicians, some teachers take requests! Or, if your teacher isn't familiar with something I mention, you may inspire your teacher to study deeper.

Those who dream by day are cognizant of many things which escape those who dream only by night.

~ Edgar Allan Poe

During what is night to most, the sage is awake; when most are awake, that is night for the sage.

~ Bhagavad Gita 2.69

Chapter 2

What is Yoga?

Dispelling Myths

Q: Isn't yoga some kind of human pretzel exercise routine for flexible people?

A: Well, there's yoga; then there's *yoga*.

Yoga has a good name. It's a millenia-old practice with great visuals and lots of cred. But the name "yoga" has been coopted by an industry in the West. In that industry, yoga is sold as a fitness product that will bring you happiness. That yoga talks like some of the yoga of the past several millenia in India, but looks like exercise, is done sporting expensive spandex-hemp blend outfits and exposed tattoos, requires sweat, physical prowess, and dramatic flexibility.

I'm talking about authentic yoga, which is much more than exercise, and shares many similarities with aspects of art.

The moment between two breaths is the moment between two thoughts. That moment is yoga.

~ Alan Finger

When Monet painted the haystacks, …
he was interested in the series … And he was interested in the thing *between the paintings.* That's important. Conservators are interested in the painting itself, but I am more interested in *the between* the paintings.

~Anslem Kiefer

If you have only seen — or practiced — yoga as a routine where people do postures, or *asana,* to use the *Sanskrit*[2] name, you're missing the big picture, just like if you viewed a postmodern work of art without any context.

Real yoga includes eight branches of practice, only one of which is asana, that work holistically to produce positive shifts in your life. Real yoga is a practice described in all the classical literature as a way of bringing together the disparate parts of yourself — reconnecting what dealing with day-to-day life has scattered. Let's look at that in a little more detail. There are essentially three parts of yourself:

It is self-evident that the whole is greater than the part

~ attributed to Aristotle

1) **The aspect of your thinking that deals with what you experience through your senses,** what I call your interpreter of data, or data processor. It compares what you see, hear, taste, touch, and smell to your memories and assesses its current relevance to you. This processing goes on incessantly, as long as sense data is coming in, or — and this is key — as long as sense data or related memories stimulate other

---

2   Sanskrit is an ancient language whose vocabulary is specialized to describe actions, mental states, energy, and other ideas useful to yoga.

memories and assessments. Note that we data process memories just like actual experiences.

2) **The part of your mental processes that are not related to current sensory data processing** — the part we might call inspiration or insight, which seems to motivate our intellect independent of direct experience.

3) **The vehicle that combines the mental functions and physical experience into the experience of living** — what we usually think of as the body.

We act based on our best judgement as influenced by these parts of ourselves.

We are not very accustomed to thinking about ourselves as having parts, but looking from this perspective can help you see the purpose of yoga and how it can help you as an artist. To make this less abstract, consider the examples that follow.

Come together
right now
over me

~ John Lennon

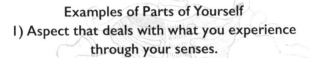

Examples of Parts of Yourself
1) Aspect that deals with what you experience through your senses.

You walk down the street. You sit on a park bench and look around. You see a man. Your internal processing begins, *"Hey, look at that old guy in the blue skullcap; I wonder why he's wearing a wool hat in July? He looks like my Uncle John. I loved Uncle John. He took me fishing. Remember when I hooked that one fish? Yuck! That's when I became a vegetarian. I need to write that article query to Vegetarian Times. I keep putting that off. Maybe I'm not destined to be a writer."* You feel an empty sensation in your stomach. The processing picks up there, weaving in what is relevant from previous processing, i.e., memories. *"I should go get some lunch. I'm going to look up a new vegetarian restaurant online, for the article, maybe. Where's my phone? … I really want to upgrade … there's the ATT store. When is my contract up? Phones are so expensive! I have to earn more money. I need to write that article query and get paid. Maybe I'm not really a writer …"*

New stimulus from outside sets the data processor part of you in motion. Once in motion, it rarely stops, because memories get triggered. We sometimes call it stream of consciousness; it's more accurately just mental chatter.

Examples of Parts of Yourself
2) The rest of your mental processes.

You're at a café. A page of notes sits in front of you. You've been working on a song lyric. Everything you've tried sounds trite or forced. The sunlight catches the leaves of the tree across the street and the flutter of the two colors of the top and bottom of the leaves grabs your attention. Your thinking pauses, and you just stare for thirty seconds. A three-word phrase moves your pen at the same moment it comes into your awareness, and in two minutes, a completely different song from the one you were working on has essentially written itself on your page.

You might label it inspiration, insight, or muse.

Examples of Parts of Yourself
3) The vehicle that combines the mental functions and physical experience into the experience of living.

You've been choreographing a piece for two hours. You're on a roll. Suddenly you feel completely defeated by a combination you're creating. The defeat moves from general malaise to a concentrated ache in the pit of your stomach. You realize that you're hungry, as you were so anxious to get to the studio that you skipped breakfast. You eat the sandwich you picked up on the way to the studio. The food tastes so good — especially the garlic mayonnaise. Even though the floor is hard, it's relaxing to sit down. You feel rejuvenated by the food. You mentally run through that challenging step while you are eating the last few bites. You stand up and your body executes the move as though you've been practicing it for days. You do it again and watch in the mirror. The shape reminds you of something your mother used to do. You begin to smile and a tear comes to your eye.

You are experiencing what could be called "in the flow."

Yoga helps you have better access to all your mental processes, to let inspiration and insight deeply influence your understanding and subsequent actions, to calm the chatter of incessant thinking. All together, that helps you live life in the flow.

Q: All this mumbo-jumbo sounds like religion or psychology. Is this Hinduism?

A: Yoga is a science — in the classical, empirical, style. A science of doing something, observing the results for oneself, noting the experience, and letting others repeat the experiment, i.e., experience it for themselves.

The history of yoga in India includes a blending of the most scientific aspects of yoga with the formation of dogma that occurs when techniques become codified and organized. Not just religions, but many yoga traditions and yoga teachers believe they have the "right" kind of yoga and the "right" way to do things. At ISHTA Yoga, we believe that everything has its place; there is no inherent right or wrong, only effects of this or that action. It's one of the tenets of the Tantra Yoga that underlies the ISHTA approach that you can find everything you need with what's here, right now. There's nothing elsewhere that's going to make the difference. That means you have what it takes in this moment, if you know how.

The good news is that you can go back to the original, Tantric approach of having the experience of yoga without any religious or school-specific interpretations. It just requires a teacher who understands the scientific reason for the practices to show you how.

Definition

What Yoga Is Not

Okay, so just to be clear, first, let's review what yoga is not. Yoga is not just exercise, it's not about being flexible or standing on your head, it's not a religion. Don't worry if you've been using yoga as exercise and you like it. You can continue, just add in the rest of yoga!

> Only union with you gives joy
>
> ~Rumi

What Yoga Is

Yoga is a practice that includes a set of tools for reconnecting the parts of yourself to restore a healthy balance. Doing so creates a shift in your life that lets inspiration and insight infuse your everyday experiences and leaves you living in the flow.

Yoga is a practice that reconnects the parts of yourself.
That creates a shift that lets inspiration and insight infuse
your everyday experiences to leave you living in the flow.

Real yoga practice boils down to three things, described here using their traditional Sanskrit names:

- **Svadyaya.** It literally means "self study." Study yoga, so you know what to do. Also, study yourself, so you see what's needed and then see how the practice is working on you. A teacher helps you learn and evaluate your practice.

- **Tapas.** It is a burning away of impurities. You take on the work that you and your teacher determine will bring you to a better state of being.

- **Ishvara Pranidhana.** It means letting the universe do its part. At a certain point when you've done your part, you need to let go. This can mean letting go of the need to have things happen your way and surrendering to the way things actually work out. Or it might mean letting that egomaniacal control freak — or the forever insecure hypercritic — step aside to allow your quiet genius to take the reigns for a while.

Row, row, row your boat,
Gently down the stream.
Merrily, merrily, merrily,
Life is but a dream.

~19th century nursery rhyme

Chapter 3

Why Do Yoga?

Creativity

Artists trade in the realm of the unique. They look for a way to make something ordinary, like paint or movement, into something that touches people in a way that surpasses the normal. In order to do that, they need to do more than just repackage ideas that their predecessors have provided. They need to grasp something at a fundamental level, and then express it from a unique or, ideally, a universal perspective. To do so leads to the outcome we call "creativity."

To find creative expression, we need to tap into our inspiration, wisdom, and intelligence, and to look via a perspective that in some way differs from the way we usually look at things.

Yoga is a practice of stopping the way we usually think in order to create a state of mind that lets in inspiration.

The role of a writer is not to say what we all can say, but what we are unable to say.

~Anais Nin

There are painters who transform the sun to a yellow spot, but there are others who with the help of their art and their intelligence, transform a yellow spot into sun.

~Pablo Picasso

Progression of Mental States
(from the bottom up)

Meditating. **Tapped into a deep source where there is no concern about blocks or lack of inspiration, but rather a trust in the part of yourself that works through your art.**

Concentrating. **Getting control over the mind's tendencies and experiencing some quiet and "spaciousness," where inspiration and new ideas have room to emerge.**

Intellectualizing. **Wrapped up in normal experience, linear thinking, anxiety; searching for answers outside or in memories.**

That inspiration fosters a flow of wisdom and intelligence in our artwork and the rest of our lives. A holistic yoga practice takes an artist through the natural progression of mental states, shown above.

Your art practice may serve as the way you progress through these states of mind to get to your creative place. I believe that art and yoga are very similar in that regard. But if you have trouble getting to your creative state of mind, yoga can be an aid that doesn't carry with it any of the baggage that your habits or history of art practice have. For example, if you are plagued by stage fright, but once you're on stage, you're fine, your art practice could use some help keeping you calm during the off-stage time. Or if you have occasional creative days after stretches of dry days, you could benefit from a more consistent route in. Yoga can help.

In his book, *Finding Your Zone,* psychiatrist Michael Lardon describes how top athletes reach a state where time seems to slow down, their minds go empty and still, then it feels like they are in the cinema waiting for a movie to begin. What they experience in their sport carries over into their other activities, too. Yoga is, literally, a practice of reaching that experience — it is training in getting "in the zone." You can use that zone for your art making.

Peter Yanowitz, drummer and songwriter for The Wallflowers, Natalie Merchant, Morningwood, and many other projects describes finding that zone in his art:

> "Drumming is like meditation. I use yoga as a way to strengthen my mind, my core, my breathing. It gives me more awareness, and I'm able to turn off my mind and let my limbs flow free."

The object isn't to make art, it's to be in that wonderful state which makes art inevitable.

~Robert Henri

Balance and Stress Relief

Stress is a drag for artists on several levels. It can make you perform poorly, leave you discontented, and contribute to ill health. Yoga works with a practitioner where he or she is to create the opposite of stress. The opposite of stress isn't just relaxing or

> Simply by showing up
> and climbing onto a
> mat, beyond mere relief
> from business as usual,
> we are offered solace,
> mammal time, and we
> leave feeling a little more
> malleable, porous, tingly.
>
> ~Debra Granik

not doing; it's balance. That balance makes your activities efficient, reducing what might have caused the stress in the first place.

Rebecca Oliveira has what many artists would consider a dream: a full-time art job with benefits! As a designer for a major brand, she draws on her art school training as a weaver to explore, sketch, and create fabrics, a job that is creative, but often stressful. She shared her experience of yoga as a way to balance out that stress, and brought up a point that many artists I speak to share: art and yoga are very similar.

> "Having to be creative in a very constrained way most of the day, yoga became my way to be [more freely] creative. The two are almost the same. Even when you're going to someone else's yoga class, you're trying to create something beautiful for yourself. That could be the way you move, or the way you breathe, or the way everything is coming together in moments of little perfection. For me, that was being creative when the creativity at work was strained.

"You're not always in perfect control of a class, but you determine your interpretation, which makes the practice beautiful for you. Everything for a little while will align in a beautiful way, and that can feel as creative as making a piece of art."

Overcoming Blocks

One of the biggest stresses for artists is blocks to creativity and performance. Actress, producer, and writer Puy Navarro describes how yoga gave her tools to expand beyond her acting and break through her obstacles to writing:

"I had always had anxiety about being still — until I realized that the best technique for me was physical theater. I had a love for and the eagerness to write, but I wasn't able to *stop* to do it. I needed to move to think. Through the practice of yoga, I was able to learn to stop, to sit comfortably … At the beginning I could sit for 10 minutes, then 20, and now, if I get in the zone, it can be for hours. Now, when I'm writing, I can be okay with the uneasiness and stay with the page — not get up and leave … I can wait until I see an image and something magical happens. Then I feel connected to the gods of theatre, the gods of writing!"

Health

In the 1970's, a Harvard researcher named Herbert Benson described what he called the relaxation response. This response moves your nervous system from the sympathetic dominance — fight or flight mode — back to the parasympathetic balance that lets your body take care of all the normal digestive and restorative functions.

Yoga provides a way to access the Relaxation Response. It also uses safe movement, strength building, coordination, and stretching, which fosters correct posture and balance. All together, yoga impacts lots of aspects of an artist's health:

- Cardiovascular health, including blood pressure
- Muscle performance
- Bone health
- Posture-related health (healthy back, neck, shoulders)
- Restorative health, which aids lymphatic function, glandular function, sexual function, vision, memory, immune system function, and sleep

A lot of people get directed to yoga when they have a physical injury, like a bad back or shoulder. As an artist, you can also use yoga to help avoid the injuries that are prevalent in your medium. For example, lots of musicians and painters struggle with shoulder, neck, and back problems.

Here's what **Benj Gershman,** bass player of the band O.A.R. said about his yoga practice:

> "Like a lot of people, I've had back issues for years. For me, these issues are not just from the way I perform with my instrument, but because of the traveling involved on our overnight bus trips from city to city over the last nineteen years. Once I developed a steady asana practice to address my personal recurring injuries, things started to shift. Now, my practice serves like preventative maintenance. And besides my daily yoga routine, there are postures great for before and after shows which benefit in the short and long term."

If you've been practicing yoga in a competitive style, where the focus is on accomplishing more and more difficult poses, your practice may be encouraging injury and imbalance rather than health. See *Chapter 3, How to Practice Yoga* for ways to make practice constructive instead of destructive.

Researchers continue to try to understand the mind-body connection and the ways yoga improves health. The U.S. National Institutes of Health even started a Center for Complementary and Integrative Health (on the web at www.nccih.nih.gov) that includes yoga research and information.

Perspective

Big Picture Perspective

Yoga is a method for breaking free of limited thinking. All the techniques that are found in yoga — postures, breathing, meditating — are designed to expand our consciousness. That can sound esoteric, or new-agey, or even delusional, but doesn't art do exactly the same thing? Yoga provides a means to tap into expanded consciousness, while art expresses what flows from that place. Most writing about the experience of yoga (union of the various parts of yourself) sounds very poetic, because it's trying to use words to describe experience beyond the ordinary, just like poets do.

… I reach what I might call a philosophy; at any rate it is a constant idea of mine; that behind the cotton wool [of daily life] is hidden a pattern; that we — I mean all human beings — are connected with this; that the whole world is a work of art; that we are parts of the work of art. Hamlet or a Beethoven quartet is the truth about this vast mass that we call the world. But there is no Shakespeare, there is no Beethoven; certainly and emphatically there is no God; we are the words; we are the music; we are the thing itself.

~Virginia Woolf

Personal Perspective & Emotional Balance

When we are faced with artistic or professional obstacles, we may need a fresh perspective — to breathe, as we often say. At other times, we could benefit from more emotional balance or stability to sustain us during tough times.

Artists need to keep objectivity when they are constantly subjected to challenges that might be considered unbearable in other fields:

- The need to prove yourself, though no one knows exactly what they want you to do and you don't necessarily know what will be successful.

- Exploring difficult topics in front of the public via your art.

- Judgement of your performance, sometimes based on a single line of dialog or melody in an audition, by others you may not know — or even respect.

- The requirement that you repeat yourself, while what inspired the work you're being paid for isn't necessarily what inspires you now.

Agatha Nowicki is an actor who works in theatre, TV, and film. She describes how yoga helps her keep perspective, given the tough issues she grapples with in her work:

"There's something very self-sacrificing about being an actor. You're constantly using the body, the emotions, the whole psyche to tell a story. Often it's a shadow story, a darker part normal people would like to avoid, but actors head straight towards it to help illuminate the human condition, to shine a light on all that suffering. You can't do that kind of thing if you don't have a center to return to; or if you don't have the strength, or the breath, to hold space for difficulty with a more expansive sense of ease supervising things. Yoga is that center. That balanced home base you return to after traveling through all those other parts of yourself. Having yoga has made me more courageous, because I know when all the heart-taxing work is done, I have legitimate tools that will bring me back home."

Body Mastery

In *Chapter 1, What Is Yoga?* I described us as having three parts:

- The part of us that processes sense data and memories;

- The part of us that brings inspiration and insight to bear on experience and actions; and

- The vehicle that carries us through experiences in the world.

The vehicle is the physical us, the body, the brain, the nervous system. This physical self is both wonderful and problematic. Wonderful, because it is interesting, useful, has sensations, and develops. It includes both mental processes and motor capabilities in a fascinating organic interaction. However, it is problematic, because it's constantly changing — aging, getting stronger or weaker, becoming injured or healing, becoming highly coordinated, hurting, feeling good.

As artists, bodies are also wonderful because they provide us a means to express the ideas that emerge from our artistic inspiration and practices. Even if you aren't a performer, at some point, you physically act to create work: pushing a paintbrush, keying a poem into a computer, crouching to get a perspective to make a photograph. Bodies can be problematic for artists when they don't function as in the past or you can't count on being able to do what you want. This unpredictability of the body can impact you mentally. The relationship between the mind and the body isn't always an easy one. For example, anxiety in the mind

While it looks from the outside like yoga is working out the body, in fact, it's helping to integrate and balance the body, the mind, and — *this is key* — the energy that enlivens and expresses through this complex vehicle.

can lead to a poor performance, even when there is no physical problem at play; or you can "power through" pain, convincing your mind it doesn't matter, perhaps paying the price later.

Yoga helps artists deal with the physical self at several levels. While it looks from the outside like yoga is working out the body, in fact, it's helping to integrate and balance the body, the mind, and — *this is key* — the energy that enlivens, heals, and expresses through this complex vehicle. Practicing yoga correctly, in the way described in the next chapter, will have you experiencing a more easeful ride in your body vehicle. You will know sooner and more clearly what you can do, you will do without extraneous worry, you'll adjust the way you use your body to minimize injuries and maximize health.

Artists who practice yoga find the nuances of effort and ease and how to move more gracefully in their bodies. They work efficiently and sense the moment when doing more is fruitless. Alan Finger likens using effort to hammering a nail. Once the nail is in, you're there — further hammering will only damage the wood.

With yourself in balance, the expression of your energy is what I've called "being in the flow." We also borrow

> Work that only comes from the head isn't any good ... You need to find a way to bring your body into your work.
>
> ~Austin Kleon, in *How to Steal Like an Artist*

> One of the greatest gifts of yoga is the deeper sensitivity to sensation it helped me develop. As I tune out the chatter of my mind and tune into my breath, I discover more and more subtle streams of the river of movement within.
>
> ~Nancy Allison

a music term to describe this state. We call it being "in tune." Artists who practice yoga flow, in tune physically, mentally, and universally. They tap their creativity and express that physically, without getting bogged down in their data processing — they just do, rather than obsessing about doing.

Travel

Travel is a part of many artists' work. If you tour, or even commute within a metropolitan area or region, that travel can start to take a toll on you physically, mentally, and emotionally. Yoga is a holistic support system. It helps by:

- Keeping your body strong, spacious, resilient.

- Giving you a way to recharge.

- Giving you a thread of continuity in the midst of changing surroundings.

- Providing techniques that you can use to conquer fear of flying, frustrations with driving.

- Training you to accept spaces of inactivity within the thrill and stress of work.

Irina Kruzhilina is a costume designer who has created major theatre, opera, and dance productions internationally, from the Barbican in London to BAM in Brooklyn to the Plovdiv in Bulgaria. Here is her description of how yoga helps her on the road:

"As an artist I travel often, and yoga has become a home. I come back to this studio, to my teaching, and it's a physical place, as well as a spiritual place. That serves as a balance that I didn't have before yoga. I also take this balance with me, anywhere I go — I remember something, or see something, or hear [Alan Finger's] voice in my head — and it draws me straight back into this feeling of home, no matter where I am in the world; this home that is a place of balance, of stability, of focus."

Chapter 4

How to Practice Yoga

Three Aspects of Practice

In *Chapter 1, What Is Yoga?*, I referred to three parts of yoga practice, as they are described in the *Yoga Sutras of Patanjali*. These parts will be fleshed out within this chapter, so here they are again for you to refer to:

- **Svadyaya.** It literally means "self study." Study yoga, so you know what to do. Also, study yourself so you see what's needed and then see how the practice is working on you. A teacher helps you learn and evaluate your practice.

- **Tapas.** It is a burning away of impurities. You take on the work that you and your teacher determine will bring you to a better state of being.

- **Ishvara Pranidhana.** It means letting the universe do its part. At a certain point when you've done your part, you need to let go.

Start Now

The goal of this book is to pique your interest in yoga and get you to begin. It's more than a pep talk and less than an instruction manual. While I'll give you plenty to get you started now, I'm intentionally avoiding telling you exactly how to practice long-term, because having *a human teacher makes such a difference* that I want you to go find one. (If you're nearby, come to ISHTA!) Imagine going to elementary school and being handed a book, or e-tablet, without any instruction. You'd stumble along — if you even bothered to keep going. The same is true of yoga. A teacher sees what's up with you and creates, then tunes, a practice to bring you to balance.

That said, start now. There will not be a better time later. Later, you will wish you had started now. I was recently teaching meditation to the faculty of an elite New York prep school. After the session, one teacher remarked to the others, "Why don't we teach this to the kids when they're little? Then they would have it in the higher grades when they're so stressed out!" Start now so you'll have it for the rest of your artistic life. Do what's in this book while you look for your teacher.

> Yoga happens in
> the now.
>
> ~Patanjali

Find a Teacher

Why Have a Teacher?

I spoke a little above about the benefits of having a teacher who can see who you are as a student and tailor a practice to bring you to balance. The Sanskrit name for a yoga teacher is *guru*. It literally means, the remover of darkness. A teacher turns on the light for you, pointing out things that are hard to see in yourself, and ways you can address them. A guru doesn't have to be from India, and the right guru may not use that title, but someone who can shed light on your practice is who you want teaching you yoga. You can study one-on-one, or take a group class. Either way, a good teacher will keep an eye on you and be available to answer questions.

Even if you have been practicing asana for a long time, your practice may simply be reinforcing your habits and imbalances. A teacher can see that, when you might be content to just keep doing what you've always been doing. A good teacher will create a holistic practice for you that helps you evolve.

Yoga was always taught by a teacher to a student. Recently, the Internet has made information on every topic accessible, and some yoga teachers, in their attempts to spread the value of yoga to as many people as possible have tried to satisfy the modern demand for video and online lessons. My opinion is that such courses are best used if you already have a teacher to confer with or have been trained as a teacher yourself. A yoga teacher might be able to process the instructions of an online course to see what applies to him or herself. It's hard for a novice to do the same. A teacher can see the student's mental, emotional, and physical condition — and the effects of the practice as he or she does it.

Practicing from a book or with a video is a hit or miss proposition, and in some cases, can be bad for you. For example, a teacher in a video might tell you to move a certain way that is outside your capabilities and causes an injury. Or you might really need to deal with stage fright, which could be addressed through breathing or meditation, and all your book is teaching you is a set series of poses that you're told to master. I lead trainings for students who want to go deeper in practice or become teachers, so they get targeted learning and mentoring from a teacher. Even those who have been practicing for years report new depths of understanding and transformation in their lives from working with a teacher in that intimate format.

What to look for in a teacher:

- Find teacher who knows all the parts of yoga.

- Choose a teacher who tailors a practice to the student.

- Look for a teacher who is humble.

How to Choose Your Teacher

How do you pick a teacher? Luckily, we tend to find key people in our lives when we're ready (yogis call it *karma*, the universe's call for *action* — film artists should like that). You will be drawn to the right yoga teacher, much as you were drawn to certain creative teachers who impacted your artistic practice.

What to look for:

• **Find a teacher who knows all the parts of yoga.**
There are eight limbs of yoga (the next section describes them). Avoid teachers who teach only asana (poses or postures), which rules out many yoga instructors, and some well-known teachers, too. It's easy to find out: ask teachers you're considering if they teach meditation in addition to asana. If not, or if they imply that's not really important until you're advanced, keep looking.

A teacher who understands asana as *part* of the yoga practice will be able to use asana as it is intended, to create a steady comfortable posture. This means more than being able to hold a handstand. It means being so balanced in your physical and emotional self that you can sit in silence, concentrate, and experience the state of stillness that will bring inspiration into your life. To do this, a teacher must understand the effects of various poses on different students. That teacher also has to know how to modify poses to suit the condition and tendencies of students to bring about the desired effect.

• **Choose a teacher who tailors a practice to the student.**
Avoid set routines where everyone is required to do the same thing. That kind of practice only works when it happens upon someone who needs it. So while you might hear someone say, "I love [some kind of] yoga," remember there are others who have left it in frustration, boredom, or even injury.

Note that you should ask before taking a class if the practice is always the same or if it takes into account different students' abilities.

Studying privately, at first, can help you figure out how to personalize your practice, and then you can decide if you want to take a group class armed with your personal training.

With a little research, you'll find the right teacher, so don't settle. For example, I started a workshop series just for men, because so much yoga is targeted to women who have the capabilities of gymnasts that men rarely have. That trend has created a situation where men are losing out on the benefits of yoga. In the workshop, I focus on moves men can make to get more balance in their bodies and end with a centering meditation to bring calm into their day. Look for a teacher who gets your issues, physically, emotionally, creatively.

- **Look for a teacher who is humble.**

  Avoid a teacher who says, "Only I have the right way" or a teacher who demands your obedience or makes you feel uncomfortable. A teacher should share energy as instruction and practice, not as power over you.

  A teacher should also respect you as an adult who knows his or her own experiences. Avoid any teacher who shows off challenging postures or bullies or embarrasses you into doing something you aren't able to do safely. If a teacher insists you do something that hurts you, gives you a panic attack, or leaves you feeling imbalanced, claiming it is "purifying," leave and find another teacher.

Once you have a teacher, you have access to his or her advice on all the various aspects of your practice. A teacher will guide you to bring you to the efficient balance that will help your life and relationships, as well as your art practice. Your initial practice may consist of doing postures with a little breathing or meditation; it will evolve as you and your teacher continue to work. Your teacher may ask you to chill out in some areas where you think you excel and try harder in others where you're challenged. If you've used the guidelines above to find a good teacher, trust your teacher's advice, even when it seems hard. That's *tapas.* Your practice will help burn away patterns that aren't serving you, on every level: physical, emotional, mental, and spiritual.

If you don't have easy access to teachers, because you live in a remote locale or travel a lot, don't be discouraged — you can find a teacher via a workshop, or by making a weekend trip to a nearby city where a good teacher lives. You may locate a teacher via the internet, but if you really can't go to a teacher, at least communicate with one via email or phone first to see if they fulfill the criterion of a good teacher. If he or she is right for you, your teacher will help you build a personal practice from a distance or recommend what video or online study might supplement your practice. Computer applications like Skype and FaceTime make it possible to have a personalized lesson from any distance.

Practicing yoga is a chance to refresh and wipe the slate and have a break that's constructive, away from trying to push something. Practicing yoga, be it meditation or asana or breathing can be a chance to get inspired.

~Rebecca Oliveira

The Eight Limbs of Yoga

Yama   Limiting actions that are destructive, such as violence

Niyama   Doing more of the actions that are constructive, such as self-study

Asana   Gaining a steady, comfortable posture

Pranayama Learning to control your energy

Pratyahara Developing the ability to stop looking outside and turning inward instead

Dharana   Developing inner concentration

Dhyana   Becoming still enough that your concentration is effortless

Samadhi   Experiencing the state where normal mind chatter gives way to an experience of consciousness itself.

Learn All the Parts of Yoga

Yoga has eight "limbs," or aspects of the practices. They are de-signed to lead you efficiently to the result: union of the parts of yourself. A teacher can help you navigate the limbs and use the practices in a sequence and/or combination that best moves you toward being the confident, creative artist you want to be. The limbs, called *ashtanga*[3] in Sanskrit, are both linear and cy-clical, that is, one helps you get to the next, but you keep doing them all as your practice evolves.

---

3   The ashtanga, or eight limbs of yoga, mentioned here are those described in the *Yoga Sutras of Patanjali*. I am not refering to the popular type of yoga practice, founded by Sri K. Pattabhi Jois, named Ashtanga Yoga.

Note that *asana,* which is the Sanskrit word for the yoga postures, is only one part of yoga. Often you'll hear people say "yoga and meditation," as though they are different. This confusion is common, because so many teachers don't include all eight limbs in their practices and consider yoga to be only asana.

When you practice all of yoga, the fruits of your practice can be brought back into your art as steadiness, energy, concentration, inspiration, and insight.

Practice Regularly

Every musician knows, practice makes perfect. Yoga practice has the same impact. The more regular your practice, the more easily your mind, emotions, body, inspiration, and creativity move in the new grooves you're creating, instead of back through the Grand Canyon of a groove you established through your life up to this point.

A little practice each day, especially of meditation, goes a long way, and the results encourage you to stick with it. More over time is better than a lot at once and giving up, so just go slow and steady. Keep studying, practicing, noting the effect. That's **svadyaya,** self-study.

Inspiration is wonderful when it happens, but the writer must develop an approach for the rest of the time ... The wait is simply too long.

~Leonard Bernstein

…you home in on your own experience and find balance that matches your nature, physically and energetically. Everyone can have the same experience of coming into tune, but it will be like the string section of an orchestra. The bass, cello, viola, and violin will all look and sound different, even though each is tuned perfectly. When you are using your yoga, your art will be flowing uniquely through your tuned instrument.

Don't Get Caught Up in Achievement

Our culture puts a premium on competition. Competition implies winners and losers. Yoga philosophically transcends competition. The *Bhagavad Gita,* a classic text on yoga, describes humans as expressions of one universal consciousness. When we experience that view, we're part of a whole, each with a role, like an actor in a play, a dancer in an ensemble, or a musician in the orchestra. Just as an actor appreciates a play from his or her vantage point, the *Gita* advises you to live life where you find yourself, doing what you think is best without feeling in competition with others.

When you practice yoga from this perspective, you home in on your own experience and find balance that matches your nature, physically and energetically. Everyone can have the same experience of coming into tune, but it will be like the string section of an orchestra. The bass, cello, viola, and violin will all look and sound different even though each is tuned perfectly. When you are using your yoga, your art will be flowing uniquely through your tuned instrument.

Nancy Allison is a dancer, choreographer, and filmmaker. She also teaches at studios and universities throughout the U.S. and abroad. Nancy describes how yoga influences her physical approach:

> "Through yoga I learned how to stop injuring myself — stop pushing too hard, egged on by ego-driven ideas of what my body should be doing, instead of what it truly needs to be doing, or not doing!"

Find Detachment

The *Bhagavad Gita* speaks a lot about your "attitude" toward what you do. We've all known people who agonize over or brag about their projects, who have dramatic fear crop up when it's time to show or perform work, who get stuck trying to make work. Others of us become wrapped up in the outcome of the work. We worry that someone will steal it; get jealous when someone else's work is recognized instead of ours; or focus on the reward (financial or recognition), and value the work based on that reward.

The *Bhagavad Gita* draws on the framework described above — one consciousness with many expressions, or players — to propose a productive attitude toward our life's work, which in your case is your art and whatever you have to do to support it. The *Gita* gives us two techniques for finding this attitude:

1) **Be an instrument.** Remember that you, yourself, are like an instrument of the universe. Take a Fender Stratocaster as a metaphor. It can't play itself, rather, it is a vehicle for the creative force that flows from the guitarist. In the same way, there's a creative force that has been pushing through the universe since the Big Bang. That force has literally brought breath into you, through evolution. That "inspiration" has put you here to make your art. Those are pretty good credentials! If you can gain that perspective, you stop questioning your abilities or, conversely, thinking you're the "genius" making your creations, and instead, you can let the universe play you.

2) **Serve others.** Krishna, the voice of the creative force of the universe in the *Gita*, realizes that it's hard for most of us to think so abstractly, so he provides a second method. To help you stop thinking about the rewards of your art, the *Gita* recommends that you do everything for

Krishna — you could think of it as similar to the spirit of volunteering, where you do things for the greater good, rather than your own benefit. Practically speaking, this could mean you do it for your band, for the play, for the school where you teach or for the people who will see your painting. It's not about changing your work to please them, it's about letting your work flow *without attachment to the results*. You make it, edit, refine, market, perform, etc., then you carry on. If someone likes it, if someone doesn't like it, if it earns a lot, if it touches 10 people's hearts or 10,000 people's hearts, it's all great and none of it defines you. Do what you have to do, let go of the results. In other words, you trust the Universe to do its part. That's **Ishvara pranidhana.**

Your yoga practice itself will benefit from the same approach. You do the practice as it's described in this book, or from your teacher. You practice with regularity and appropriate determination and you accept what comes. You see people in a class balancing on their hands and know it may or may not be in your abilities. If you and your teacher think it's a good practice for you, you try it, going step by step to stay safe. You practice for the practice, not for the achievement. If it's hard to stay abstract about it, do it for your art, your significant other (they love what yoga does to you!), your studio mate, the cast. Keep it out of the realm of thinking about it and in the realm of just doing it.

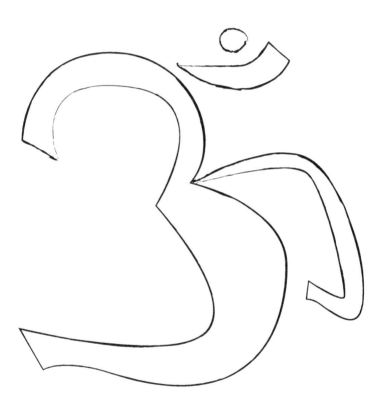

Chapter 5

What to Practice

Practice for Creativity

Meditate

The secret weapon of creativity is meditation. Meditation is the culmination of a yoga practice and brings the most concentrated form of the benefits of all the practices.

The Yoga Sutras provide a beautiful explanation of why meditation helps with creativity. I paraphrase[4] here:

When you still your thoughts, you experience your fundamental self.

At other times, you become confused about who you are, and think you are the thoughts circulating in your mind.

As an artist, creating something great requires tapping into a truth that is felt uniquely and perhaps at a level that approaches the universal. Meditation will put you in touch with the part of you that has a perspective beyond your thoughts — an inspired perspective. Otherwise, you stay stuck in replaying old experiences and rehashing the same thoughts. So much art feels like a rehashing, because it comes from similar experiences and the same thoughts about those experiences. Take for example the work of a new band that is trying to "make it" by imitating what's currently popular. Compare that to a band that does a unique remake of an old song. The former sounds like someone

---

4   The paraphrase is of Sutras I.2-4.

else's idea; the latter *is someone else's idea*, but sounds like something new.

You may stumble upon the "great idea." You may spontaneously have a meditative experience, and a unique, universally-felt metaphor or melody or gesture may come to you. Meditation's role is to put the machinery for having that experience on line and at your command. Whereas before you waited for "the muse" to pay a visit, with a meditation practice, you walk right into her living room and sit down.

Having this kind of access to your creativity brings a confidence that will ripple through your work and the rest of your life. Instead of fretting and sweating over every step of art making or performing, you can focus on crafting your flow of ideas. If you have challenges with presenting or performing work, you will start to see the causes of your fears with more clarity and reduce and eliminate them. Instead of bringing stress and anxiety and irritability into the rest of your life, you can give your art its due and balance your personal life and relationships.

Meditation can seem overwhelming — the idea of stilling one's thoughts can be daunting. But if you allow for the stages of meditation to unfold,

> There is a vitality, a life force, an energy, a quickening that is translated through you into action…
>
> ~Martha Graham

> The artistic journey is the surrender into the space of stillness where the grace of wisdom of whispered answers can be heard by the heart.
>
> ~Shailly Agnihotri

meditation is just a natural process that we, in our noisy, distracted lives, have stopped making time for.

So you know what to expect, here are the four states of mind you will experience over time. They are the final four limbs of the ashtanga:

• **Sensory withdrawal** (*pratyahara* in Sanskrit). Most of us have lots of experience of this stage occurring naturally. It happens in sleep, when noise or someone tapping us doesn't register. It happens when we are daydreaming and are oblivious to our surroundings. It happens when we are extremely focused on something and don't hear a colleague calling us or we miss our subway stop.

• **Concentration** (*dharana* in Sanskrit). The act of focusing the mind narrows the wide-ranging thinking that our mental processor is capable of. In that narrowing, we start to shift mental gears away from that rehashing part of the mind that is so dependent on sensory input. You may have noticed that extreme focus (another way to say concentration) was listed in the previous bullet as a cause of sensory withdrawal — the two work together. You will focus on something at this stage: your breath, a phase (*mantra*), or an image, and keep going back to it when you get distracted.

• **Effortless concentration** (*dhyana* in Sanskrit). You take the initial steps — you withdraw and concentrate. Then you stop needing to try to concentrate, your mind just does. If you continue to surrender into that object of concentration, you cross into the part of your consciousness that overarches your daily thinking. Note that you become effortless *after* your initial effort. If you haven't prepared well enough through the first two stages — pratyahara, turning away from the distractions your senses offer and then concentrating your mind so it goes into the dharana stage — then that concentration can't become effortless; your mind will just go on a stream of consciousness joyride. But if you practice regularly, concentration that was hard at first becomes easy.

- **Samadhi.** There's no satisfying English word for this, so I'm just going to use the Sanskrit. *Samadhi* is a state of being conscious, but not engaging the activity of thinking in our normal way. It's somewhat like being asleep, but still aware. The *Yoga Sutras* describe the first taste of Samadhi as a recognition of yourself as consciousness — the thinker, rather than your thoughts — and "being" in that state for a period of time. In ISHTA Yoga, the period we aim for is 18 minutes, long enough to shift your mental state like a period of deepest sleep. An immersion in your still consciousness opens the channel of creativity, wisdom, and insight.

Any amount of meditation begins the process and starts the flow of benefits. The experience of all four steps begins with you sitting down to meditate now.

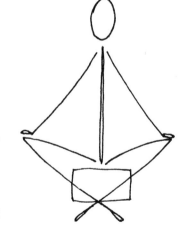

A journey of
a thousand miles
begins beneath your feet.

~Lao Tzu

Sample Meditation: apa japa

A good teacher (see *Chapter 3, How To Practice Yoga*) will help you find the right meditation to suit your personality, your current condition, and your goals. Here's a basic meditation technique that can get you started. It's called apa japa at ISHTA Yoga, but you may have heard it called vipassana or mindfulness in other meditation traditions.

1.) Find a comfortable, steady seat. Sit on the floor, if you have the capacity to do so comfortably. If not, raise your seat relative to your crossed ankles so your legs extend level to your hip joint. Use a bolster, blocks, a pillow, or even a chair to suit your body. Sit up tall, not slouched.

2.) Begin to observe your breath. Follow the inhale and the exhale. The breath is now your object of concentration. If your concentration strays, bring it back to the breath. Let your breath do whatever it wants, you are not regulating it. Through concentration for a period of time, your breath may start becoming softer.

If it gets very soft, like a puff of air, let your attention move into the middle of your brain — the middle of your mind — and surrender there. The surrender is like the letting go you do when you're ready to go to sleep. Stay there as long as you are comfortable (or a little longer, if you're trying to build to 18 minutes). Use a timer, or download a meditation timer app so you don't have to keep wondering how long it's been or coming out of meditation to check your watch.

Mantra

Mantra is the use of the vibration of sound to shift the vibration of your thoughts, much like a painter adds a bit of paint to tweak a color on the palette. To use a mantra, first do the meditation above. Then when you are quiet and calm, repeat the mantra, first aloud, so you feel the vibration, then silently, so the transformation occurs at the subtle levels of your mind. Repeat the mantra 3 times aloud, then 9 times silently. Once you have done this for a month, you can call on the mantra any time during your day to help you bring about the effect.

Mantra is most powerful when you hear it aloud first from your teacher, which is called being given or initiated into a mantra. Your teacher's voice sets you correctly in the vibration. You can contact me to be given a mantra if your teacher is not familiar with this practice.

> You recharge, in the way of imagination. You know, sometimes our vases get empty. We can go into an artistic training, or take workshops — or we can do yoga and that ... fills you up every time, so you're never empty.
>
> ~Irina Kruzhilina

Sample Mantra: Saraswati, *for inspiration*

The mantra below is a call to attune your mind to the energy of expression and to let your expression be filled with inspiration and wisdom.

Om Aim Saraswatie Namaha,

which is pronounced:

oh-m…ah-eem…sah-rah-swah-tee-eh-ee…nah-mah-hah

Practice for Stress Relief

Use your Breath: Pranayama

The breath is a bridge connecting the normal thinking state of mind to the meditative state. Using breath intentionally to change your energy and state of mind is a great practice to have available, because it's so convenient — you can breathe any time you need to make a shift. In Sanskrit, regulating your breath and its corresponding energy, or prana, is called pranayama. Pranayama is an excellent tool for dealing with stress, because it's active. While meditation is also good for stress, sometimes if you're too stressed out, it's hard to get quiet enough to concentrate. Let pranayama serve as the first step.

Sample Pranayama 1: belly breath, *for calming*

1.) Lie on your back. (If you cannot be on your back, or want to use it during a performance or audition, try to have an upright posture that allows your abdomen to be free to move with your breath.)

2.) Inhale and exhale normally a couple times and watch where your breath fills your body.

3.) Slow and extend your breath as much as is comfortable.

4.) Let your inhale move your belly, like you're filling it up with air (of course, air only goes into the lungs, but your diaphragm pushes down the intestines and abdominal organs to make the belly appear to inflate).

5.) Let your exhale lower your belly back in.

Even though you may feel some expansion in your chest or back, try to focus the expansion in the belly. Repeat 9-12 times, until you feel calmer.

Sample Pranayama 2: alternate side breathing *for balancing*

1.) Find a comfortable, steady seat.

2.) Turn your palms face up on your knees. Make a gentle fist with your right hand.

3.) Visualize your breath entering through your left hand, up your arm and into the left nostril. Close your left hand into a gentle fist. Hold your breath for a moment.

4.) Gently open your right hand as you visualize the breath leaving the right nostril and flowing down the right arm and out that hand. Breathe back in through the side you just breathed out (in the hand, up the arm, in the nostril). Hold a moment, then release and visualize the breath leaving the opposite side.

5.) Continue breathing out, then back in, on one side; then switch to go out and back in on the other side.

Repeat about 6 cycles. This pranayama can be very quieting. It can leave you a little withdrawn or "spacey," so be sure you feel back to normal before going back out into your day. (Use one or two asanas to get grounded.)

Use your Body: Asana

Getting into your body with the focus of a yoga asana practice is a powerful way to alleviate stress. I see dozens of people each week who use the combination of asana, pranayama, and meditation as their method of keeping on an even keel in the hustle-bustle of New York City. To paraphrase Sinatra, if you can beat stress there, you'll beat it anywhere.

For stress relief, steer your asana practice toward poses that leave you feeling restored and balanced rather than challenged and "pumped up."

Practice for Health

A Holistic Practice

I hope you're starting to get the idea that all the practices are good for everything. From the perspective of health, that's certainly the case. I'm going to talk about asana in this section, because of the obvious connection to the body. But in the medical field, there's growing use of meditation to improve health as well. All the aspects of your self are connected and work together.

How to Approach Asana

In the Yoga Sutras, asana is defined simply as a comfortable, steady posture. In the Middle Ages, Tantra yogis began using physical poses, as well as pranayama, to alter their energy to foster powerful meditations. While some asana is centuries old, much of the asana you see today was designed in the early 20th century to give teenage boys a way to burn out their physical energy in a disciplined way. Many American practitioners have cherry picked that asana and called it "yoga," separating it from the rest of the practices. I hope I've convinced you that you'll get the most out of yoga by including all of it.

I am not my body. My body is nothing without me, that's the truth of it.

~Tom Stoppard, in *Rock and Roll*

When it comes to using asana for health, it's vital that you avoid thinking that poses are something you're supposed to master and work through like a series of karate belts. Instead, asana works to physically shift the flow of energy through our channels of prana to create balance. That balance of forces within us — active-passive, dense-light, strength-flexibility — leaves us with physical health, emotional and physical gracefulness, and an ease at dealing with life's challenges. You need a customized practice that suits you to achieve that balance.

I'm a fountain of blood
In the shape of a girl

~Björk, in "Bachelorette"

If tailoring practice to you, instead of having you conform with a practice's rules, seems the opposite of what you learned from your prior classes or instructors, you're not alone. Most of the students I train to become teachers are constantly asking me, "Is it right to do it that way?" to which I reply, "It depends." To help illustrate the historical validity of the individual approach, consider the lineage of Tirumalai Krishnamacharya. This revered teacher who lived in Mysore, India revived a general interest in yoga there in the early 20th century. Three of his students subsequently became the heads of schools that are well-established in the West.

- **Pattabi Jois** was the guru of the Ashtanga Yoga school. The Ashtanga Yoga practice is fixed and vigorous. Students progress through a primary and advanced series, tackling challenging postures with goals for correct alignment. Poses are often connected by active transitions on the breath, which is called *vinyasa.*

- **T.K.V. Desikachar** was the guru of the Viniyoga approach. His school promotes a completely individualized approach with an emphasis on breath and little emphasis on challenging poses or specific alignment. A practice includes repeated movement into and out of a pose to encourage full breathing.

- **B.K.S. Iyengar** was the guru of Iyengar Yoga. His school promotes an extremely methodical emphasis on aligning the body in specific ways in poses and has no emphasis on breath in asana. Poses are held stationary for extended periods.

Why are these three practices from the same teacher so different? Because Krishnamacharya gave individualized practices to his students, including these three. These dynamic yogis were motivated by the benefits they witnessed from their given practices, refined those practices, and started schools based on their own uniquenesses. The founders of these schools have now passed on, but the schools and their approaches remain. Teachers within those traditions are sometimes not aware of the broader spectrum of yoga that emerged from Krishnamacharya. Also, like many instructors, teachers from these schools may not be versed in the eight limbs discussed in *Chapter 3, How to Practice Yoga.*

As I noted in Chapter 3, a teacher who understands the effects of the poses, and not just how to do them, will keep you safe and help you meet your goals. I once had a student in a class who looked like he might be a teacher; his physical expression of the poses was perfect. He confided in me after class that he was a ballet dancer, so doing the poses was easy enough, but he had no idea what he was doing or why. It's not accomplishing the postures, but doing them as a way to help integrate the three aspects of yourself that is important. It's hard to do that if you're just trying to make shapes with your body. Find a good teacher to help you practice well!

The sample poses below are fairly safe for anyone. You can do them to get a taste of asana, or ask a teacher to include them in your practice. (As I mentioned in Chapter 1, yoga teachers, like musicians, often take requests!) Even if you've been practicing for a long time, and these poses seem simple, try them with a more comprehensive focus on breath, concentration, and alignment to get a better sense of the whole of yoga. Many teachers I know enjoy beginner classes just as much as advanced classes, because the yoga is the same regardless and beginner classes give them more time and space to feel the effects of poses.

Props:

You can try yoga in a class or with a teacher without buying any-thing, but if you're going to practice yourself at home, you need a few props:

- a yoga mat
- a blanket
- 2 blocks
- a strap
- a bolster (optional)

Use a mat designed for yoga. Yoga mats provide traction that keeps you from slipping. Also, for stability, practice in bare feet rather than socks. Shoes don't allow enough articulation of the parts of your feet for yoga, so leave them off. Use a blanket or a folded towel under your knees if they are sensitive when on the mat. You can also use the blanket or blocks to raise your hips when you sit.

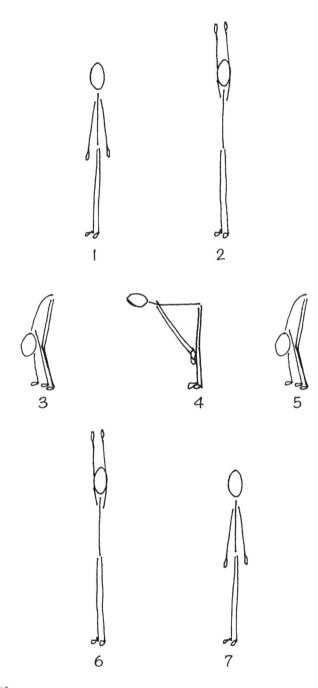

Sample Asana: sun breath

This simple set of movements on the breath can calm you when you're nervous, invigorate you when you're lethargic, and keep you in a balance between striving and giving up. Each movement happens on a part of the breath, as indicated below.

1. Stand with your feet parallel, pelvis neutral, chest open, arms by your side (Mountain Pose).

2. As you inhale, take your arms in an arc out to the sides and up overhead.

3. As you exhale, fold forward, bending your knees so your belly can rest on your thighs. As you reach the limit of your forward fold, lift your sit bones to bring a stretch to the back of your legs (my wife once called this last bit "mooning the sky," and that image always makes me smile). If you have a lot of range in your hamstrings, your legs might come straight doing this, but it's very rare. If you feel discomfort in your upper back, set your hands on blocks.

4. As you inhale, keep your legs and hips the same, but lift your chest halfway up, to where your back comes flat. Draw your shoulder blades together slightly to broaden across your upper chest.

5. Exhale back into the forward bend, same legs and hips (knees bent, moon the sky).

6. As you inhale, come all the way back to standing, arms circling up, palms facing or touching overhead.

7. Exhale and return your arms back by your sides to Mountain Pose.

Repeat the cycle of poses on your breath, which is called vinyasa, in Sanskrit, 3-6 times.

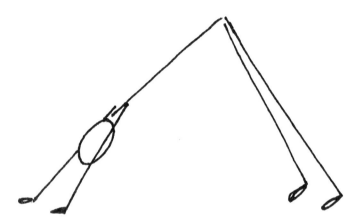

Sample Asana: downward-facing dog, *for artists who get stress in their shoulders and back*

A lot of artists rely on their bodies in their art-making and performance. When you're trying to make something work, you don't always think about your postural alignment or efficient ergonomics. For painters or sculptors who are always reaching their arms, for string players, for computer-based artists or writers, and for dancers, just to name some, downward-facing dog can be a great shoulder opening posture with the added bonus of putting your back and neck in a bit of traction to relieve stress and realign.

Note: If you have a wrist or shoulder injury, check with a teacher who can work with you personally on this pose.

1. Start on hands and knees.

2. Before you move, press securely into your fingers, especially the index and thumb. Rotate your upper arms to bring the biceps a little more forward. (If your elbows hyperextend, put a micro-bend into them so the muscles of your arms work to support the joints.)

3. Curl your toes under and, keeping your knees bent, lift your hips toward the upper corner of the wall behind you. This should create a straight line from your wrists through your shoulders to your sit bones.

4. Keep that long line in your upper body and hips, then push down through your heels, only until your hamstrings resist. Completely straightening your legs here is a bad idea for almost everybody — it usually makes you round your lower back and often hurts your wrists.

Hold 5-7 breaths and then lower back down onto all fours.

…when you add in
the breathing and core
strengthening, you can
transcend to a whole
new level of drumming
and expression.

~Peter Yanowitz

Sample Asana: blown palm, for artists who rely on their breath

I'm not implying that some people don't need to breathe, but many musicians and actors rely on breath to make their art. This posture helps you access expansion in your side ribs. Since we all do need breath, this is a fine practice for anyone!

1. Stand with your feet parallel, pelvis neutral, chest open, arms by your side (Mountain Pose).

2. Inhale and take your arms up overhead. Interlace your fingers except for your index fingers, point the index fingers toward the sky.

3. On your next inhale, lift through your ribcage and extend up and over to one side, like you're leaning over a barrel. Only go as far over as you can go while maintaining strength through your core abdominal and back muscles, instead of feeling like you're hanging over. If your breath feels constricted, come back up until your breath feels expansive. Let the inhale and exhale move you a little — the inhale will naturally lift you up; the exhale will naturally lower you further into the side bend. Come back to center and repeat to the other side.

Sample Asana: eagle, for dancers

Dancers use their bodies in complex ways. Many dancers end up in yoga, because their kinesthetic skills are a great match for asana. Dancers need to remember to balance strength with their flexibility, as many dancers have dramatic range of motion in parts of their bodies. This will often mean holding a pose at a level that is before their extreme limit, where they might tend to hang on ligaments or lean into joints. I taught an aerial performer with a contortionist's flexibility, who would literally pop her femur out of her hip socket to go further down in triangle pose until I instructed her to stop before that point and stand strong instead. Dancers often are called on to externally rotate their thighs to create second position steps and they are encouraged to project their ribcages forward. The eagle pose works to balance both thigh rotation and ribcage position.

1. Stand in Mountain Pose with a low block next to your left foot. Pick a point ahead of you and focus your gaze there throughout the pose.

2. Bend your knees slightly and lift your right leg across the left at the thighs. Place the ball of your right foot on the block.

3. Inhale and open your arms wide to the side; exhale and cross the right arm under the left in front of you. Bend your elbows and wrap your forearms around each other, maybe bringing your palms to touch. Allow your shoulder blades to get a stretch away from the spine. If it brings a stretch and not a stress in your shoulders, lift your arms so that your upper arms move toward parallel with the floor.

4. Find stability in your standing leg and try shifting weight out of the foot on the block. If you can lift it off the block, balance there or try hooking your toes behind the calf of your standing leg.

5. Keep your balance on one leg as you unwind your arms and legs. Lower with control to Mountain Pose.

Do both sides, hold each as long as you have control, up to 5 breaths.

Practice for Perspective & Balance

See Things as They Are

Life is full of challenge.

The Buddha called this idea the first Noble Truth (the concept is called *duhkha,* in Sanskrit, and is often translated as "life is suffering"). Unlike some "positive thinking" programs, yoga doesn't try to convince you that life is actually a bowl of cherries, and you're going to get rich or be successful or be permanently happy if you do these X steps. It's pretty obvious if you look with discernment, that life falls squarely in the Drama genre. Life is full of tragedy, sadness, joy, transcendence, and every other possible dramatic element. It's my personal belief that life is, literally, a great stage drama in which we are all players. Oh wait, I guess that was Shakespeare's idea, first. Oh, and also Virginia Woolf's, per her quote in Chapter 2. And it's the metaphor behind yoga's Shiva Nataraj, the cosmic dancer.

This should be a relief for those of you who like to draw on angst or emotional pain for your art! None of that drama is going anywhere soon, even though we hope we're evolving toward a more enlightened world.

Instead of trying to convince you that life is actually something it's evidently not, yoga helps you become wiser, clearer, and more intuitive, which will help you be more graceful in dealing with life's challenges. Through gaining more perspective on your circumstances, the tools of yoga help you change your relationship to the inevitable problems life presents. Where you used to feel helpless and burdened by life's challenges, you will find that you have the power within to address those challenges. Sometimes addressing them dissolves the challenge; at other times, it means you see things in a new light that makes difficulties easier to take on.

All the practices of yoga help you gain perspective. The most powerful is meditation, because it literally changes your way of thinking. Pranayama can bring emotional balance that helps you when challenges arise. And once you have a little more perspective, even asana practice helps, by serving as a laboratory where you can start to understand and work with your tendencies in dealing with challenges.

For example, imagine you are a perfectionist about your performances and are never content, even when audiences are moved and approve. When you get to your yoga mat, you might bring the same perfectionism to the postures, looking unrealistically to match up with someone in a picture or in the yoga studio. If you have a good teacher, he or she will guide you into versions of postures that work perfectly in your body to bring balance, energy, strength, and spaciousness. In realizing that your version is where the perfection lies, you can start to trust your artistic performance as well.

I practice yoga as a way to maintain and charge my body spiritually, emotionally, and physically. It balances the weight of life into release and momentum, and reminds me that there is always a way through, no matter how painful it is. It brings joy and creates space for celebration, makes my body and mind stronger and more flexible, and also provides a sense of well being.

~Melissa Staiger

Sample Mantra: Ganapataye, *for breaking through obstacles*

We have tremendous internal resources. That fact inspires many works of literature and film. When a protagonist like Ulysses — or Katniss Everdeen — runs into impossible odds, rather than giving up, he or she calls on some inner strength to pull through. Using yoga, you can attune to the determination and persistence you need to overcome challenges with the following mantra. (See the section *Practice for Creativity,* above, for guidelines on using mantra.)

Om Gam Gam Gam Ganapataye Namaha

which is pronounced:

oh-m…gah-m…gah-m…gah-m…gah-nah-pah-tah-yay…nah-mah-hah

Get Inspired

Yoga tradition includes a number of texts and an iconography that generations have turned to as reference for everything from how to practice and live to a philosophical and mythological framework describing the universe.

If you are so inclined, you can take a look at the *Upanishads,* the *Bhagavad Gita,* or stories about yogis (probably the most well-circulated is Paramahansa Yogananda's *Autobiography of a Yogi*). If you're not inclined to read yoga philosophy, that doesn't matter at all. Practicing, not reading, is what makes a difference, just like in art. An artist might make a great art critic, but becoming a critical theory major doesn't necessarily make someone an artist. In the *Bhagavad Gita,* Krishna states explicitly that your experience from practice makes the writings superfluous:

> "When your intelligence has passed out of the dense forest of delusion, you shall become indifferent to all that has been heard and all that is to be heard [from the yoga writings]." (*Bhagavad Gita*, 2.52)

So if all the yoga speak and Sanskrit and philosophy turn you off, get your inspiration from practicing. If your teacher is requiring you to do otherwise, look for a teacher who gets you, and leaves out the talk, and helps you keep practicing instead. Just remember that practicing includes all eight limbs!

The world itself is inspiring, and you may find yoga gives you a new way to appreciate it. I have been spending time lately looking at what theoretical physicists are saying about some of the same topics covered by yoga philosophy. It's remarkably similar! Notions of the Big Bang, where everything comes into being from nothing, including all the laws of Nature pervading everything, could be lifted right out of the *Upanishads*. Just looking up at the night sky can expand your perspective.

Once you begin to practice this centuries-old tradition, you might be inclined toward the philosophy as a way to gain a better understanding of the things you're feeling. Philosophy is ultimately just someone's attempt to describe the reality we're all experiencing.

You might find yoga itself to be a source of inspiration in your artwork. I have written three novels exploring ideas I first considered in yoga philosophy. A student once gave me a copy of his latest rock CD that included a clever lyric about shaking your seven chakras. Another student who was a painter made a series of abstract paintings based on the five elements yoga describes as making up the universe. Another student who is a singer-songwriter made a video casting herself as a deity from the yoga pantheon. A student who is a photographer shot a haunting series based on the myth behind the Virabadrasana, or Warrior, poses. Way back in 1970, George Harrison drew on yoga inspiration for the #1 hit, "My Sweet Lord," about Krishna, the voice of wisdom in the *Bhagavad Gita* — and yoga's name of the laws of Nature, or the intelligence that pervades the universe.

Yoga relaxes and focuses my mind allowing thoughts, emotions and intuitions to arise and mingle in playful and really useful ways. It helps me turn creative dreams into artistic realities.

~Nancy Allison

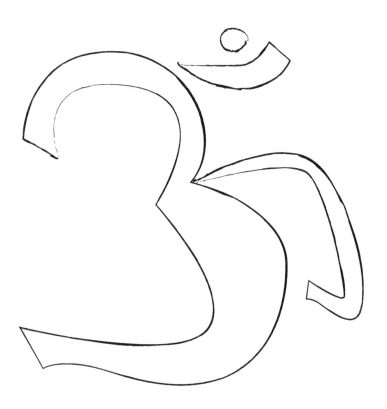

Chapter 6

What Now?

The Journey Begins

As Lao Tzu's comment in the *Tao Te Ching* is often paraphrased, the journey starts with a single step. It's up to you now to take that step. Many artists, probably some you know, use the eight limbs of yoga to help them with their creativity, health, sanity, and perspective. I hope I have inspired you to test for yourself this powerful set of tools. I trust yoga will support you as you pursue the noble path of giving expression to the unique vision of the artistic soul.

Start with the beginning practice at the end of this chapter. Look for a teacher who can guide you and tailor practice to you.

A consistent yoga practice will lead you to a state of mind where your thoughts get quieter and even pause, leaving you with a new perspective beyond everyday chatter. From that vantage point, your work will be inspired and meaningful.

Yoga is also inspiring for my work. In yoga, we are working with the geometry of the body, but also the fluidity of emotions, sweat, and tears, at times. My belief is that this is directly connected to my artmaking process and supports it. Sometimes, a powerful experience in yoga inspires me to create a painting or drawing. At other times, the effects are more subtle and help my overall well being, because I have to feel well to make great art.

~Melissa Staiger

Your emotions will be less likely to rule you. You will have confidence around your creativity and balance in your life.

Elizabeth Gilbert, author of *Big Magic* and *Eat, Pray, Love,* said in a TED Talk that along the way, artists lost the notion of the artistic soul as connected to a source of inspiration. She explained that ancient Romans used the word "genius" to mean the divine spirit who came and assisted an artist. She continued, saying the modern perspective, that the artist *is a genius,* places overwhelming pressure on artists, and that we need to get back to thinking of art as being a combination of our work and the genius coming through our efforts to make art.

> Yoga helps me tune in to what is necessary and tune out what isn't necessary, so that the dance can dance me.
>
> ~Nancy Allison

Yoga can help you connect to that universal genius, your source of inspiration; to move gracefully through the challenges of making your work; and to realize your role as the embodiment of what yogis call Lila, the great dance of life.

Namaste.

A Beginning Practice

Here's a basic 20-minute practice to use while you look for your teacher.

Sun Breaths, 5 rounds
(see page 54)

Blown Palm, 2 times each side
(see page 58)

Downward-Facing Dog, 5 breaths
(see page 56)

Eagle Pose, once on each side
(see page 60)

Goddess Pose, 3+ minutes

Set a bolster onto a low and high block (see side view, left). Roll a blanket or towel lengthwise. Lie back on the slanted bolster with knees bent and feet together. Wrap the blanket over your feet and under your legs, so your legs are supported. Turn your palms open on the floor. Relax.

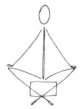

Apa Japa Meditation, 3+ minutes
(see page 47)

Savasana, 3+ minutes

Lie on your back with palms turned toward the sky and legs released so your feet rotate open. Let your mind go still; just take a rest.

ISHTA Yoga

ISHTA, the Integrated Science of Hatha, Tantra, and Ayurveda, is a holistic system of yoga designed to bring balance and grace into every moment, providing unbound potential for you to express your uniqueness. By tailoring practice to each individual, ISHTA Yoga helps students transform in ways that feel constructive and supportive. This makes the practice appropriate for everyone, regardless of strength, flexibility, size, shape, habits, tendencies, history, and goals. In other words, it's for you. More information at www.ishtayoga.com.

If you liked *Yoga for Artists*

Peter Ferko teaches ISHTA Yoga classes, workshops, and trainings. You can find out when he's teaching and also find his books, music, and art projects at

www.peterferko.com

Read more by Peter Ferko

Peter's fiction is influenced greatly by his art and yoga practices. Check out these novels that are tailor-made for artists, yogis and other thinkers!

Incarnation, a novel

Incarnation follows a journalist, an actor, a writer, and a programmer whose dreams and desires play out together on the global stage, again and again. Each time, they find meaning as they spin on life's mysterious wheel of fortune.

The Black Hole of the Heart, a short novel

Three characters' stories intersect around the similarity of emotional upheaval and the mysterious phenomenon of the black hole. With irresistible pull at play, each falls and then finds a new truth about the possibilities of ending, rebirth and the power of love.

Wally and Kali, a novel

A poignant tale of love, family, and Tantra in which a sometimes clueless Wally tries to navigate a nudist ashram, the Brooklyn artist's life, and his new stepson's teen angst.

Notes on the Artwork

All yoga posture illustrations are by Rebecca Oliveira. The drawing of the Sanskrit Om is by Peter Ferko. Cover art is by Peter Ferko. The author photograph on the back cover is by Alan Finger.

Several historical pieces of art are used as backgrounds for text boxes:

Three of those illustrations are from *The Medicine of Akbar*, Anonymous Persian Anatomical Illustrations (Iran or Pakistan, ca. 1680-1750) National Library of Medicine.

The other is by Malar Ragini - "Krishna Playing the Flute to Seven Gopis Holding Musical Instruments," from the *Ragamala Series*. Kotah, OK. 1760. Cleveland Museum of Art.

Printed in Great Britain
by Amazon